THE VICTORIAN [illegible] SERVANT

Trevor May

Dinner in the servants' hall. The servants' meals were bound by conventions of etiquette as strict as those observed upstairs. Customs might vary in individual houses, but seating was according to a definite hierarchy. Lower servants knew better than to strike up idle conversation, although the atmosphere became more relaxed when, after the meat course, the upper servants withdrew to the housekeeper's room (sometimes known as 'Pug's Parlour'). Illustration from George R. Sims, 'Living London', 1901.

Shire Publications

CONTENTS

Cover: Male servants at Petworth, West Sussex, in the 1870s. The picture includes a steward, footmen, chefs, lodge keepers and butlers. © NTPL

British Library Cataloguing in Publication Data: May, Trevor. The Victorian Domestic Servant. – (Shire album; 338). 1. Domestics – Great Britain – History – 19th century. 2. Great Britain – Social conditions – 19th century. I. Title. 640.4'6'0941'09034. ISBN 978 0 74780 368 3

Published in 2012 by Shire Publications Ltd, Midland House, West Way, Botley, Oxford OX2 0PH, UK. Website: www.shirebooks.co.uk

Printed in China through Worldprint Ltd.

It is not always possible to tell who was a domestic servant and who was not, as is exemplified by this photograph, taken in the mid 1870s outside the Plough public house at Elstree in Hertfordshire. It is partly a question of definition, since domestic servants might also assist with their employer's business. Some of these maids may have been chambermaids at the inn, and the woman second from the right in the middle row (Isabella Jones, the author's grandmother) was not a domestic servant at all, but the daughter of the publican. Yet, like many of her class, Isabella assisted with at least some of the domestic chores and clearly did not feel above being photographed with her father's employees. (Author's collection)

INTRODUCTION

When in 1959 an obscenity case was brought before the High Court against the publishers of *Lady Chatterley's Lover*, the prosecution (which failed) was not helped when one of the leading counsel asked the jury if this was the kind of book they would wish their servants to read. Presumably this senior member of the legal profession still employed a servant. According to the Ministry of Labour, there were still 30,000 men and 275,000 women (including daily helps and gardeners) employed in 'private domestic service' at that date. The real heyday of the domestic servant was certainly past; yet even today it is not so far distant as to prevent anyone who digs a little into his or her family history from finding evidence of close ancestors on one side or other of the master–servant relationship.

Interest in the world of 'Upstairs, Downstairs' was reawakened with the great success, in both Britain and the United States, of the television series of that name (1970-5). In addition to their grand family rooms, more and more country houses began to open to the public those rooms 'behind the green baize door' that formerly acted as the power-house, ensuring that the domestic lives of the well-to-do should run as comfortably and smoothly as possible. When in the 1970s the National Trust opened Erddig, a country house in North Wales, the official visitors' entrance to the house was made through the servants' quarters.

Group photographs of servants often depict them holding tools or something else associated with their occupation. This photograph, dating from 1852, shows the servants of the Yorke family of Erddig, near Wrexham in North Wales. The cook-housekeeper, the butler, the head carpenter and the coachman are readily identifiable from the brace of fowl, the cork-screwed bottle of wine, the saw and the whip respectively. (© National Trust – Erddig)

In 1851 there had been over a million servants in Britain, making domestic service the second largest occupation after agricultural work. Not only were a vast number of people thus employed, but the range of households in which servants were to be found was very wide indeed. At one end of the spectrum were aristocrats, such as the sixth Duke of Bedford (died 1839), who employed 300 servants, or the sixth Duke of Portland, who employed 320 at the turn of the twentieth century. At the other end were thousands of clerks and other lower-middle-class families who employed a single maid-of-all-work. Mr Pooter, in George and Weedon Grossmith's comic novel *Diary of a Nobody* (1894), had his Sarah, who may not have amounted to much and who caused him endless heartache, but who at least placed him in the servant-keeping class. Writing in the last year of Victoria's reign (1837-1901), the social investigator Benjamin Seebohm Rowntree suggested that the keeping of servants marked the dividing line between the middle and the working class, but this view neglected the fact that many artisans and other members of the working class employed domestic help (to act as child-minders, wash clothes or do 'the rough'), and that even some of these servants lived in.

The size of servant establishment depended on the size of a person's income, and there were many manuals (including the ubiquitous one of Mrs Beeton) that set down expected norms for different levels of wealth. In 1857, for example, J. H. Walsh advised in *A Manual of Domestic Economy*:

'An income of £1,000, clear of all other expenditure, and devoted solely to housekeeping and rental, will afford the following servants: 1st, a butler, or manservant out of livery; 2nd, a coachman or groom; 3rd, one or two housemaids; 4th, a cook; 5th, a lady's maid, or a nursery maid, or sometimes both.... The income No 2 [this was his £500 a year class] will only afford three servants, viz. 1st, a page, or a general manservant, or a parlourmaid; 2nd, a housemaid; and 3rd, a cook. This provides also for the keeping of a single horse or pony and carriage. If, however, the family is a large one, a young lady's maid must be kept for the purpose of making their dresses at home, and in that case a horse cannot be afforded... The income No 3 [£250 a year] will not allow even of the above domestics, and a maid-of-all-work must be the means of doing what is required, aided in some cases by a girl, or in others, by the younger members of the family... The income No 4 [£100 a year] is barely sufficient to provide what is required for the family in the shape of lodging, food and raiment, and therefore no servant can be kept, or at all events, only such a young girl as it is quite useless here to allude to.'

We have to take such manuals with a pinch of salt, however, for the historian

Two servants of widely different ages at a Suffolk country rectory. Between 1881 and 1901, while the percentage of girls between fifteen and nineteen in domestic service fell by 7.3 per cent, that of women over forty-five rose by twenty per cent – a reflection of the fact that alternative employment was begining to attract younger women. The maid with her broom is clearly not going to let the young man in until he has scraped his boots. 'General lads' performed a variety of jobs both inside and outside the house and were the male equivalent of the maid-of-all-work. (Suffolk Photo Survey, Suffolk Record Office: SPS 6838)

Edward Higgs reminds us that 'To fall back on the evidence of manuals of domestic economy... is equivalent to using *Vogue* to reconstruct the lifestyle of the "typical" modern family. Such manuals reflect the aspirations, if not the daydreams, of Victorians, rather than the detailed workings of their homes.'

How did masters and mistresses view their servants, and how did servants see themselves? What were conditions like in the servants' quarters; and what were the duties that different members of a domestic staff undertook? These are some of the questions to be examined in the following chapters.

Male servants at Petworth, West Sussex, in the 1870s. From left to right: (back row, standing) the assistant under butler, a footman, the under butler, another footman, the steward; (middle row seated) a lodge keeper, the chef, another lodge keeper; (front row, sitting on the ground) a footman, the steward's room man, the second chef, another footman. The exalted status of the steward is confirmed by the fact that he does not wear livery. (By kind permission of Lord Egremont)

THE RECRUITMENT OF SERVANTS

In the middle ages servants often came from the same social groups as their masters. By the nineteenth century this was no longer the case, with the possible exceptions of the steward of a large estate or the governess. The latter filled a most unenviable position in the household, being neither true servant nor true member of the family, but falling uncomfortably in between.

In the nineteenth century most domestic servants were of humble origin and, in the early Victorian period at least, were from a rural background, for country girls and boys were considered more tractable and industrious than their urban counterparts. As Cassell's *Family Magazine* put it in 1878, 'We cannot but regard the agricultural class as the best from which to draw the average servant; and we have hopes of the continuity of the supply, if we can only impress upon this class the value of domestic service in contrast with that of many other competing occupations'. The supply did continue, but largely because most of the new employment opportunities were in the towns and cities, while the range of jobs in the countryside continued to be limited.

OUR MAID-SERVANTS.

Mistress (opening Post-Bag). "FOURTEEN LETTERS FOR YOU AGAIN TO-DAY, MARY! I CAN'T UNDERSTAND IT."

Mary. "WELL, MA'AM, I OUGHT TO HAVE GIVE YOU NOTICE, BUT I HADVERTISED. YOU SEE HOW GOOD SERVANTS IS SOUGHT AFTER."

From the eighteenth century advertising i newspapers was a means of engaging domesti servants and was described by Mrs Beeton a 'one of the commonest modes' by the late 1860s. The cartoon is from 'Punch', 18th Sep tember 1875.

The first rung of a life of domestic service might well be a place in a local household, and here personal recommendation or knowledge of the applicant's family was crucial. Some employers, however, were suspicious of taking on local girls for fear that they might run home, draw 'followers' after them or convey gossip back to the community. The parish clergyman, local squire or respected tradesman was often a point of contact for both local and more distant jobs, and this power of patronage reinforced deference towards such members of the community amongst labouring people.

A traditional place for domestic servants or agricultural labourers ('servants in husbandry') to find employment was the hiring fair, or 'mop' fair. It was mainly dairy maids who presented themselves there, although some cooks and housemaids did so. Just as the shepherd carried his crook, so the cook would

AS LADY's-MAID, or to wait on two young ladies, a person, aged 24. Understands her duties, having four years' good character, the lady being in town. Address, post paid, M. K., 5, Motcomb-street, Belgrave-square.

AS LADY's-MAID, or to Attend on Young Ladies, or as Needlewoman, a respectable young person. Understands dressmaking, hairdressing, lace joining, and transferring. Can be well recommended. Direct to W. T., Mr. Coleman's, baker, Liverpool-road, Islington. No objection to the country.

AS LADY's-MAID, a highly respectable person, who can speak Italian, has been accustomed to travel, and understands dressmaking and hairdressing: wishes for a SITUATION to travel on the continent. Good references can be given. Direct to A.Z., 15, post-office, Charing-cross.

AS COMPANION, or Nursery Governess.—A young lady, age 20, wishes to obtain a SITUATION in either of the above capacities. She is acquainted with the rudiments of an English education, and is a good needlewoman. No objection to travel. Address to E. H., 9, Church-street, Manor-place, Walworth.

AS HOUSEKEEPER, or to Superintend the Kitchen in a nobleman's family, or as professed Cook and Housekeeper in a quiet family, a person who understands her business in all its branches, with several years' high character from a nobleman's family. Address L. L., Mr. Barrett's, 63 and 64, Piccadilly.

A YOUNG ENGLISH PERSON, who speaks French like a native, wishes to obtain a SITUATION as NURSE, Lady's-maid, or Teacher in a school. No objection to travel or to the country. Address, post paid, to E. T., 10, Finchley New-road, St. John's-wood.

A PERSON, who has travelled and speaks French, is desirous of meeting with an ENGAGEMENT as COMPANION to a lady; or in a family travelling preferred. She would not object to the charge of children, and has excellent references. Address J. C., 7, Frederick-terrace, St. Leonard's-road, Bromley, Middlesex.

A LADY, going to Germany, in a fortnight, WANTS a HOUSEMAID to accompany her. She must be a thorough servant, and understand needlework. None need apply with less than two years' good character, with a reference in London. Call at 43, Clarges-street, Piccadilly, between 10 and 12, on Thursday, the 7th instant.

AS good COOK, a middle-aged person. She understands the duty of a kitchen. Or to a single gentleman, where there are one or two more servants kept. She can have a good character from the place she has just left. No objection to a short distance out of town. Direct to A. K., Mr. Browning's, post-office, Conduit-street, Westbourne-terrace, Hyde-park.

A LADY is desirous to obtain a SITUATION for a respectable female as ATTENDANT on an invalid or aged lady. She can be strongly recommended by the family in whose service she has lived for many years in a similar capacity. For particulars apply, either personally or by letter, to Mrs. James Murray, 2, Vanbrugh-terrace, Blackheath.

A Respectable YOUNG PERSON wishes for an ENGAGEMENT as LADY's-MAID, or Young Ladies'-maid. She is an excellent needlewoman, dressmaker, hairdresser, and can get up fine linen. She can speak French, having received an excellent education. Has an excellent recommendation. Direct to G. Y., Mr. Gascoyne's, hairdresser, Bruton-street, Bond-street.

AS PROFESSED COOK and HOUSEKEEPER, in a nobleman's or gentleman's family, a respectable, steady, active person, who has a thorough knowledge of French and English cooking and confectionery, and the management of a family with economy, and has filled similar situations in families of distinction.—D. A., Warder's, 61, Great Marylebone-street, Portland-place.

Advertisements from 'The Times', 7th July 1853.

Left and below: *Servants seeking employment at a London registry. Servant registries had existed since the eighteenth century, when they were considered as little more than pimping establishments. Between 1907 and 1910 the London County Council secured powers to license and regulate such agencies, but elsewhere their control remained patchy. Photographs from George R. Sims, 'Living London', 1901.*

hold a basting spoon and a housemaid a broom, the distinction between the two kinds of domestic servant also being reinforced by the wearing of red and blue ribbons respectively. Hiring fairs, which had something of the atmosphere of a slave market, were in decline by 1850, although they remained significant in some areas (including Wales, the south of Scotland and the north of England) and had not disappeared before 1914.

By the latter part of Victoria's reign most large towns had one or more servant registries. Many were run as private businesses by women (for example, widows who needed a means of maintaining themselves), and a few became large establishments. A particularly well-known one was that run by Mrs Hunt in Marylebone, where in the 1890s and early 1900s, according to F. V. Dawes, 'servant girls newly arrived from the country slept in the attics, like disposable stock, while waiting to be placed'. Some

registries were run by charitable agencies such as the Girls' Friendly Society, founded in 1874, or the Metropolitan Association for Befriending Young Servants. By the mid 1880s the latter charity had twenty-five branch offices and claimed to be placing five thousand pauper girls in employment annually.

The workhouse was also a major source of domestic servants. Workhouse girls were often thought to be well trained, but though they were accustomed to hard work they had no experience of handling delicate or costly items. 'Better' families therefore tried to avoid them, and it was among artisans and others at the bottom end of the servant-keeping class that they were most likely to find work.

No one was likely to employ a servant without an interview, although it did not necessarily take place with the employers themselves. In larger houses it would usually be the housekeeper who had the responsibility of appointing and dismissing female staff (other than the cook or ladies' maids), while the butler did the same for the indoor male staff.

There tended to be a high turnover of staff. In 1876 it was estimated that in London ten per cent of female domestic servants were looking for a new situation. A more recent study centring on Ashford, Kent, found that of 312 servants enumerated in the census of 1841 only seven were with the same family by the time of the 1851 census and only one stayed in the same household from 1841 to 1861.

Sometimes servants moved because of disagreements with their employer; in other instances it was in order to secure a promotion. Whatever the reason, the servant needed to take a good 'character' or reference. This necessity gave the employer considerable power, for not only was there no obligation to provide a reference at all, but a false or defamatory one was only actionable at law if the servant could prove express malice, which it was virtually impossible to do.

'A Girl before and after Reclamation.' The engravings are based on photographs commissioned by Dr Barnardo about 1870. Such pictures were intended to loosen charitable purse-strings, but in 1877, after allegations that the pictures were unfairly posed (one was found by the courts to be 'artistic fiction'), the practice was stopped. Children's homes and workhouses provided a steady stream of young girls for domestic service, often in the households of artisans and others of limited means. From 'The Graphic', 16th January 1875.

PAY AND CONDITIONS

Establishing what a servant might have earned in the Victorian period is no easy matter because there are so many variables. Household accounts, advertisements in such newspapers as *The Times* and schedules in household manuals can all be used as evidence. The schedule included in the 1861 edition of Mrs Beeton's *Book of Household Management* can be taken as a starting point and indicates some of the complexities. Firstly, and not surprisingly, it can be seen by comparing the wages of butler and housekeeper (generally the two senior servants) and male and female cooks that men's wages tended to be higher than women's. It is also evident that monetary payments were dependent on the nature of other allowances made, or whether a male servant's livery was provided (once again, women were at a disadvantage in that their pay was lower, *and* they were generally expected to provide their own uniforms). There were also regional differences. Mrs Beeton observed that her figures were those current in or near London, but, as Charles Booth indicated thirty-five years later, rates differed even within London. Booth concluded, for example, that the average annual wage of a housemaid was £17 in the West End of London but £13 in the East. This no doubt reflected the size of establishments in different parts of the metropolis, for it was generally held that the larger the servant establishment the higher the average wages paid. Physique could also be a factor determining pay, especially in the case of footmen. A good pair of calves was an important requisite, and extra inches in height meant higher pay. At the end of the nineteenth century £20-£22 a year was the going rate in London for a footman measuring 5 feet 6 inches (1.676 metres). At 6 feet (1.829 metres) he might have expected £32-£40.

Monetary wages alone do not give an adequate picture of the rewards enjoyed by servants in comparison with other workers. Perquisites also have to be considered, as well as the value of food and accommodation to those who lived in. Perhaps the best-known perquisite was the cook's right to any dripping or bones, both of which could be sold to dealers. There was also a trade in candle

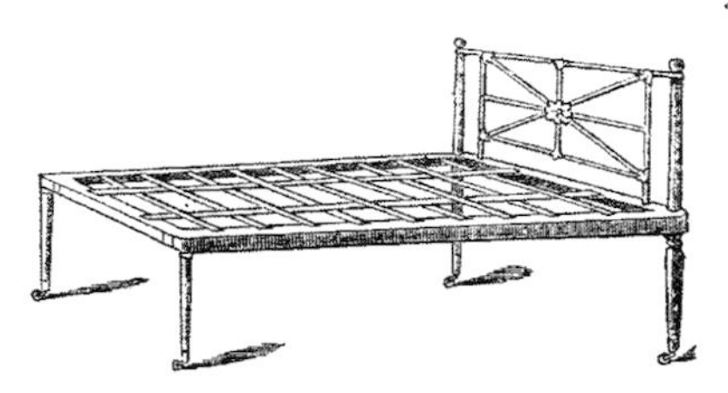

Furniture suitable for servants' rooms. Engravings from Cassell's 'Household Guide', c.1870. The accompanying article observes that 'A servant's bedroom should have as few articles in it as are consistent with comfort', and it was held that 'the less carpet laid on the floor ... the healthier and freer of dirt it will be.' The condition of servants' rooms is evident from the advice that 'From wooden bedsteads insects may... be wholly extirpated by washing in strong brine and boiling water. The skirtings and cracks in the walls, doors and window frames, also need the same process.'

Right: *Cartoons in 'Punch' were rarely sympathetic to servants. It is therefore difficult to conclude that this comment on their accommodation was meant to be ironic. From 'Punch', 8th July 1865.*

Below: *Whatever else servants lacked, there was never a shortage of improving homilies. This example comes from 'The Parish Magazine' of 1873. (Author's collection)*

WHAT WILL BECOME OF THE SERVANT-GALS?

Charming Lady (showing her House to Benevolent Old Gentleman). "THAT'S WHERE THE HOUSEMAID SLEEPS."
Benevolent Old Gentleman. "DEAR ME, YOU DON'T SAY SO! ISN'T IT VERY DAMP? I SEE THE WATER GLISTENING ON THE WALLS."
Charming Lady. "OH, IT'S NOT TOO DAMP FOR A SERVANT!"

A Good Servant.

A Good Servant.

WOULDST thou a household servant be,
Three points of character I see
Needful for thriving,—these the three:

Be sober, honest, and discreet,
Or no good mistress wilt thou meet;
And be in person clean and neat.

Three things avoid with special care:
Tales from your master's house to bear,
For once out they fly everywhere;

Avoid strong drink, for none can know
How fast the love of it may grow,
And then disgrace will not be slow;

Scraps give not to your friends away
Unless your mistress says you may—
Their greed will grow till it betray.

Three things in household service too
'Twere well that thou shouldst ably do,
Though *all* may be well done by few:

Scrub well, cook well, and well attend,
Then will thy mistress be thy friend,
And make thee happy in the end.

Scrub well the floors and make them white,
Polish the tables, shining bright,
Rub all the glasses clear as light.

With noiseless step and watchful eye,
Whate'er the guests may want supply,
Making no bustle needlessly.

Still three rules more must thou observe
If thou perfectly wouldst serve.
And praise and honour well deserve:

If you do wrong the error own,
Nothing hide that should be known,
Or conceal what should be shown.

Never let idle vanity
Tempt you your ladies' clothes to try,
Or in their drawers and cupboards pry.

Let all things in their places be,
That none need seek what all should see;
And aim at punctuality.

Such, then, as all these things can do
We reckon servants good and true;
Pity there should be so few!

ends and old bottles, and the benefits of this fell to the butler. It was usual for a lady's maid to be given her mistress's cast-off clothing (and at her death she might expect to inherit the whole wardrobe, with the exception of items of lace, fur, velvet or satin). Even the coachman had his 'perks', which included the right to any old wheels – provided only that he had been in service with the family as long as the wheels had been! Perquisites were a frequent cause of friction, being open to conflicting interpretation. Some servants placed a very broad construction upon the term, exemplified by Thackeray's comic character Charles J. Yellowplush, a one-time footman and general manservant: '[W]e'd the best pickens out of the dinners, the livvers of the fowls, the force-mit balls out of the soup, the egs from the sallit. As for the coals and candles, we left them to the laundrisses. You may call this robry – nonsince – it's only our rights – a suvvant's purquizzits is as sacred as the laws of Hengland.'

Servants might legitimately expect to dine on some of the leftover food that had been prepared for consumption 'upstairs', although more expensive items were reserved for the family to eat the following day, either cold or as the basis

IMITATION IS THE SINCEREST FLATTERY.

Nurse. "I wanted to go into Town this Afternoon, if you could spare me, to get a new Bonnet. And—I admire your Taste in Bonnets so much, Mum, I was a-thinkin' I couldn't do better than go to the same Shop! !"

Above and right: *Domestic servants were readily criticised for any tendency to rise above their station. Here, the nurse desires a bonnet like that of her mistress, while the main concern of the lady's maid is that a dress which will probably be given to her as a perquisite should not become damaged. Cartoons from 'Punch', 1876.*

"CHACUN POUR SOI."

Lady's-Maid. "I beg pardon, Ma'am, but your Dress is trailing—hadn't I better loop it up before you go out?"

Lady. "No, thanks, Parker, I prefer letting it trail, as it's the Fashion just now——"

Lady's-Maid. "Yes, Ma'am—but as the Dress is to be *Mine* some day, I think *I* ought to have some say in the matter!"

of another dish. As with many aspects of the domestic servant's life, it is difficult to generalise about the meals that they consumed, although there is widespread agreement that they ate at least as well as most members of the working class and enjoyed more meat than others of a similar station. However, a butler wrote in 1892 of the 'course abundance' of food, where quantity was not matched by quality. He pointed out that many cooks did not see the preparation of servants' meals as part of their brief, so that it was often left 'to the tender mercies of the kitchen maid'. The result was that a badly cooked joint was frequently served up, to reappear again and again at mealtimes, 'till someone, nauseated by its continual reappearance, chops it up and assigns the greater part to the swill-tub'. It was in such households that servants were more likely to help themselves to tit-bits returning from their employer's table.

Most housekeeping manuals intended for mistresses stressed the importance of economy, although rich employers hardly needed such books unless they were misers, but there were some writers who encouraged a more benevolent treatment of servants. A lady writing in *Longman's Magazine* of May 1893, for example, observed:

> 'It is whispered that in some houses servants' bedrooms are lamentably ill-arranged and furnished. Time and money are spent in drawing-room gimcracks which impede movement and attract dust, whilst cracked looking-glasses, broken basins, and, worst of all, bad bedding, prevail in the unseen sleeping-rooms. Sordid ways, too, as regards food are not unknown. It is a very wholesome thing to fast and abstain oneself, but not to impose fasting or abstinence on our dependants.'

Servants were never allowed to forget their dependence. The attitude of many Victorians towards their servants was the same as their attitude towards children or even animals. One manual of the 1880s pursued an equestrian analogy. The reader was enjoined, 'You are mistress absolutely'; and although she was advised to be 'kind, just and equable' with her servants, she was also warned to 'hold fast the reins in your own hands'. At least one maid, according to John Burnett, recalled a prospective employer actually asking her to open her mouth so that her teeth could be examined. Servants were subjected to their employer's discipline and, like children, were weighed down with petty rules – especially in the case of girls and young women. Pains were taken to discourage 'followers', both on grounds of morality and in order to avoid the spread of gossip about the activities of the household. When 'downstairs' had its own access to the street via a door into the sub-pavement area it was difficult to prevent visitors. Many a policeman on the beat found warmth and comfort in the servants' kitchen. One mistress, finding herself short of small

E. S. Turner wrote that the numerous servant handbooks published in the nineteenth century, especially for women, were as likely as not to tell servants 'on one page how to preserve their virtue, on the next how to preserve fruit'. 'Kitty: A Pastoral' (1886) is an example of the cheap romantic fiction that maids no doubt enjoyed, much to the irritation of their mistresses. Kitty starts off as a country girl, becomes a maid, falls in love with her mistress's son and ends up as Countess of Masborough. In real life she was much more likely, if she failed to 'preserve her virtue', to be dismissed without a reference. (Author's collection)

"Who's there?
Nay, answer me,
Stand, and unfold thyself!"
Hamlet.
Tommy Atkins! Housemaid Betty!
Be on the alert, I pray!
Don't you see that Captain Pipeclay
now is coming down this way?
Betty clutches, in her hurry, the
rifle with which Tommy shoots,
Tommy, likewise in a flurry, with
his Betty's broom salutes.
Comus.

A snatched kiss leads to the guard being changed in an unexpected way. Especially in the vicinity of barracks, soldiers proved such notorious 'followers' of female domestic servants that people talked of the scourge of 'scarlet fever'. Nursemaids, who were often found walking with their charges in the park, were thought to be at particular risk from the attentions of off-duty soldiers, although it was a risk that they perhaps bore with equanimity. Illustration from a Victorian Christmas card. (Author's collection)

change, called down the stairs, 'Have you any coppers there?' 'Yes, Ma'am', confessed the cook, 'but they're both my cousins.' Servants resented their loss of freedom, and this, as much as anything, made alternative employment attractive wherever it was available. It was not the work itself that they found degrading; there is ample evidence that many servants took an enormous professional pride in performing it well. The bitterest pill to take was the necessity of adopting a servile attitude towards their employers.

Deference was due not merely from servants towards those for whom they worked but also from servants at the bottom of the domestic hierarchy to those at the top. A commentator in 1900 wrote of servants that 'their minds are saturated with the idea of social grades and distinctions; they will not even live with one another on terms of social equality'. The major divide below stairs was between 'upper' and 'lower servants', the former being those who had most personal contact with their employers. They were visibly distinguished from their subordinates by the fact that they did not wear livery. However, they could easily be told apart from their employers, not only by their demeanour, but also by certain subtleties of dress, such as the butler wearing the 'wrong' tie (a black one) with his evening dress, or the lady's maid wearing a dress that had gone out of fashion.

On large country estates the upper servants were headed by the steward, whose role was that of a manager or agent. In smaller establishments, especially urban ones, it was the butler who reigned supreme. Other upper servants included the housekeeper, the children's nurse, the lady's maid and the cook. Lower servants included the footmen, parlourmaids, housemaids, kitchen maids,

The housekeeper was at the very apex of the hierarchy of female servants. Her ever-present bunch of keys was a token of her trusted position. The telltale jangling, it has been suggested, has secured for housekeepers an unassailed position in the ranks of Victorian country house ghosts! Engraving from 'Heads of the People', c.1840, by Kenny Meadows (1790-1874). (Author's collection)

THE HOUSEKEEPER.

For pickling, preserving, and cookery, none could excel her. She prided herself, also, upon being an excellent contriver in housekeeping.

GOLDSMITH.

laundry maids and those who assisted them. Forms of address between servants marked these social distinctions. The butler was addressed as 'Sir' and the housekeeper as 'Madam'; and young servants were also expected to use these forms when addressing their seniors. Whether married or not, cooks and housekeepers were always referred to as 'Mrs', while ladies' maids and governesses were given the title 'Miss' by those beneath them. These differences of status could give rise to bad feelings. Ladies' maids in particular often seem to have aroused resentment because of the airs and graces they gave themselves.

THE WORK OF MALE SERVANTS

'In all establishments it is [the butler's] duty to rule.' So said one of the countless domestic handbooks that appeared in the nineteenth century. In many households the butler was an awesome figure, not only to the subordinate servants but even to the mistress and sometimes, no doubt, to the master too. Excessive pride was considered to be the failing of many. So was insobriety. The latter charge is a plausible one, even if unsubstantiated. The butler's role in a household was an ancient one, and his title derives from the Old French *bouteillier*, meaning a servant

LICENCE FOR ONE MALE SERVANT, 15s. 0d. BU 1146

* Viscount Enfield

of Dancers Hill in the Civil Parish or Township of South Mimms within the Administrative County † of Middlesex is hereby authorized to employ ONE MALE SERVANT from the day of the date hereof until the *31st day of December* next following; the sum of FIFTEEN SHILLINGS having been paid for this Licence.

Granted at South Mimms this 6th day of January 1914 by George Hollis

*Note—Name to be inserted in full.
† If the residence is within a County Borough strike out "Administrative" and insert "Borough" after "County".
S.D. 1912.

Licence for a male servant. The necessity to purchase this was imposed in 1777 in order to help allay the cost of the American War of Independence. In 1785 female servants were also taxed, but so great was the outcry that the decision was repealed seven years later. The tax on male servants was eased throughout the nineteenth century but it was not abolished until 1937. In addition, hair powder, used to adorn liveried footmen and coachmen, was taxed between 1786 and 1869. (Author's collection)

who looked after the bottles and casks. Overseeing the wine cellar continued to be the butler's responsibility, and he was expected to be skilled in the bottling and decanting of wines, as well as in their general care. If beer was brewed, the task of managing it also fell to his lot. Even more valuable than fine wines in many cases was the family plate, which was also in the butler's charge. If there was a plate room it was likely to be close to the butler's pantry, and either he or a footman was expected to sleep close by. Together with the footmen, the butler waited at table, and overall responsibility for the arrangements rested with him. It was he who announced in the drawing room that all was ready. Few butlers of any experience would

The 'tiger' was a liveried servant, generally a young lad, who rode behind while his employer took the reins and held the horse's head when his master alighted. Whereas footmen were valued for their height, 'tigers' were appreciated for their diminutive size. From 'Driving' in the 'Badminton Library' series, 1890.

Those who could not afford to employ a footman or who needed extra help for special occasions could always engage a temporary man to wait at table. Greengrocers seem often to have fulfilled this role, although 'The Servant's Practical Guide' of 1880 did not encourage this: '[The] traditional greengrocer from round the corner or a waiter from a confectioner's, are not the best class of waiters to employ for the purpose, or from whom good waiting is to be expected; servants out of place, personally known to the butler, or persons who have formerly been gentlemen's servants, are most to be depended on.' This cartoon from 'Punch's Almanack', 1876, is titled 'Gentlemen Helps' and the caption reads: 'Comely Greengrocer (who waits at Evening Parties, to Lady Customer). "Shall I 'ave the pleasure of meeting you this evening at Lady Fitzwiggle's Ma'am?"!!'

'There is something awe-inspiring to me about an English butler,' runs the caption to this illustration from 'Penelope's Experiences in England', written by the American writer Kate Douglas Wiggin (author of 'Rebecca of Sunnybrook Farm') and published in 1900. It was not merely foreigners who might feel intimidated. 'The Servant's Practical Guide' observed that it was not unknown for a butler to be so consumed with pride that 'the mistress ... stands greatly in awe of him, and hardly ventures to invite a guest to dinner without giving him full notice of her intention'.

The butler's pantry at Uppark in West Sussex. On the table cutlery is laid out ready to be cleaned. On the left is a closet bedstead which at night could be placed across the doorway to the strongroom. On this a footman would sleep in order to keep guard. Male servants often slept downstairs, sometimes because of a lack of suitable bedroom accommodation, but also to place them as far away as possible from the female domestics sleeping in the attic. (National Trust Photographic Library/ Nadia MacKenzie)

have needed the injunction set out in the *Servant's Practical Guide* of 1880 that the form of words should be 'Luncheon is served' – '[he] does not vary this sentence for the sake of variety'. A butler might, on occasion, be allowed to think for himself, but not to speak for himself.

The butler's job was no sinecure, and it was more likely to be the footmen who were work-shy. A *Punch* cartoon of the mid century has the lady of the house saying, 'Oh Thomas! Have the goodness to take up some coals into the nursery!', to which the footman replies, 'H'm, Ma'am! If you ask it as a favour, Ma'am, I don't so much object; but I 'ope you don't take me for an 'ousemaid, Ma'am!' While not condoning such attitudes, Mrs Beeton could understand them. She warned that 'when the lady of fashion chooses her footman without any other consideration than his height, shape, and tournure of his calf, it is not surprising that she should find a domestic who has no attachment for the family, who considers the figure he cuts behind her carriage, and the late hours he is compelled to keep, a full compensation for the wages he exacts, for the food he wastes, and for the perquisites he can lay his hands on.'

Someone treated as an object, she argued, could not be expected to behave as a rational and moral being. And she was correct in her assessment that footmen, perhaps more than any other servants, were regarded as conspicuous symbols of wealth. That this was so is clear from the elaborate and expensive liveries that they wore, both inside and outside the house. No woman servant could compete with this display. The cost of footmen (whose livery was generally provided by the employer), together with their inflexible attitude towards work, was among the reasons for the relative decline in their numbers. Some estimates reckon that at the beginning of the century female servants outnumbered males by just under eight to one, whereas the 1881 census showed that by that date there were twenty-two women servants to every man. By 1900 all but the grandest and wealthiest households were replacing footmen with the much less expensive parlourmaid.

When performing any of his public duties, whether in dining room, drawing room or hall, the footman, observed Mrs Beeton, should be 'attentive to all... [but] obtrusive to none'. He was expected to move effortlessly and silently, speaking to no one unless spoken to, deaf to all conversation and with shoes that did not commit the 'abomination' of creaking or squeaking.

REFLECTED GLORY.
Shopman. "HERE! HI! ARE YOU HIS GRACE THE DUKE OF BAYSWATER?"
Magnificent Flunkey. "I HAM!"

This cartoon from 'Punch', 18th August 1883, captures well the haughtiness often attributed to footmen. In the servants' hall visiting servants were referred to by the title of their master or mistress.

The footman, 'a young and stately creature, leaning on his "staff of office" and complacently waiting his lady's orders', is illustrated in this engraving by George Cruikshank, 1829. A footman was originally an outdoor servant who walked or ran alongside his master's or mistress's horse or carriage. The full livery worn by a footman was an extravagant display of his employer's wealth and harked back to the clothes worn by a gentleman in the previous century.

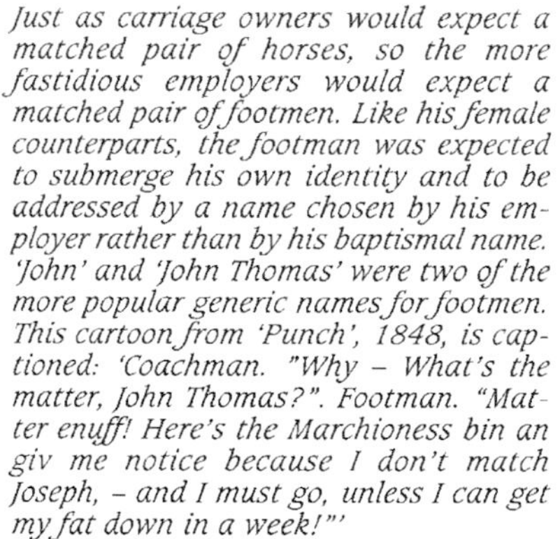

Just as carriage owners would expect a matched pair of horses, so the more fastidious employers would expect a matched pair of footmen. Like his female counterparts, the footman was expected to submerge his own identity and to be addressed by a name chosen by his employer rather than by his baptismal name. 'John' and 'John Thomas' were two of the more popular generic names for footmen. This cartoon from 'Punch', 1848, is captioned: 'Coachman. "Why – What's the matter, John Thomas?". Footman. "Matter enuff! Here's the Marchioness bin an giv me notice because I don't match Joseph, – and I must go, unless I can get my fat down in a week!"'

If not undertaken by a footman, boot-cleaning was often the job of a boy. The machine illustrated here was designed not so much to ease his burdens as to prevent the insides of the boots from becoming soiled by dirty hands. Mrs Beeton stressed, 'Much delicacy of treatment is required in cleaning ladies' boots, so as to make the leather look well-polished, and the upper part retain a fresh appearance, with the lining free from handmarks, which are very offensive to a lady of refined tastes'. In early Victorian times blacking might have been prepared at home, one recipe including ivory black, treacle, spermaceti oil and white wine vinegar. Later on it was more likely to come from a branded bottle. Illustrations from Cassell's 'Household Guide', c.1870, and from a trade catalogue of 1893.

Shoes indeed featured largely in the footman's work downstairs, as it was his responsibility to clean the footwear of all members of the family, together with those of their guests, unless there was an under-footman or a boy to do it. Footmen also daily cleaned, trimmed and filled the oil lamps, of which there might be twenty or more in a large house. Longleat had five hundred; while at Belvoir Castle in the 1830s some six hundred gallons of oil were consumed in a season of about four months. Lamps were stored on shelves during the day, partly because of the fire hazard but also because those with glass founts were prone to expand unevenly in sunlight and crack.

Any large house was likely to have rooms or areas dedicated to particular cleaning tasks, for, as the architect Robert Kerr put it in 1864, 'Every servant, every operation, every utensil, every fixture should have a right place and no right place but one'. The extreme was perhaps reached at Kinmel, Scotland, which had a room set aside solely for the ironing of newspapers, a task thought necessary to set the ink and prevent it from rubbing off on patrician hands.

THE WORK OF FEMALE SERVANTS

Footmen may have been expected to move silently, but housemaids were meant to be invisible, and all cleaning jobs had to be performed either before the family got up or while they were absent. As one housemaid later wrote, 'It was assumed, I suppose, that the fairies had been at the rooms'. Ideas as to the supposed frailty of women might have been challenged by the sight of the heavy work done by housemaids, and their 'invisibility' meant that no gentleman was likely to encounter a maid with a heavy coal scuttle or hot water can and feel impelled to offer a hand. Some employers took this state of affairs to extremes. It was stipulated at Crewe Hall, Cheshire, that no housemaid was ever to be seen, other than in chapel, while the tenth Duke of Bedford (died 1893) was liable to dismiss any maid who unwittingly crossed his path after midday, by which time all housework was supposed to have been completed.

So much work had to be done before the family was up and about that housemaids were obliged to rise very early. Mrs Beeton commented, 'The housemaid who studies her own ease will certainly be at her work by six o'clock in the summer, and, probably, half-past six or seven in the winter months, having

The maid of all work, illustrated in an engraving by Kenny Meadows in 'Heads of the People', c.1840. While her costume is similar to that of the maid shown on the cover of this book, she is far too busy to be coquettish. (Author's collection)

spent a reasonable time in her own chamber in dressing. Earlier than this would, probably, be an unnecessary waste of coals and candle in winter.'

The first task of the housemaid in winter was to open all the downstairs shutters and take up the hearth rugs in the rooms that she was going to clean before breakfast. She would then start with the breakfast room, sweeping the dust towards the fireplace. On a cloth placed over the carpet she would place her box, into the bottom part of which she put the cinders (to be recycled in the kitchen or laundry) and in the top of which she kept the brushes, blacklead, emery paper and cloths needed to clean the grate.

Fire-lighting was an art, and an experienced housemaid was expected to manage the task using no more than seven pieces of wood. Maintaining the fires in a house was also a test of strength, for an establishment employing eight

Manuals of etiquette insisted that guests should be allowed to bathe in their rooms if they preferred, even if there were bathrooms in the house. Some people considered that bathrooms were fit only for servants. The fantasy of soaking in a bath in front of the fire may still have its appeal, but the reality was that the comfort was purchased through the hard labour of a housemaid loaded down with buckets of water. The photograph shows a charcoal-heated bath in the Silk Dressing Room at Tatton. (National Trust Photographic Library/Andreas von Einsiedel)

Left: *'Servants of the Wrong Sort', from 'The Graphic', 21st December 1878. Finding fault with servants came easily to many employers. Illustrated here (clockwise from top right-hand corner) are: the maid who does not stay up for the return of her master and mistress; the maid who makes indiscreet remarks to visitors about the cleanliness of the house; the cook who does things 'her own way'; the clumsy housemaid; the maid who laughs at table talk; the maid who asks for time off; the nurse with more of an eye for a column of soldiers than for the child in her care; the housemaid who reads private correspondence; and the over-zealous duster.*

Above: *Many servants must have been almost perpetually tired. This was most especially the case with the housemaid, much of whose work had to be accomplished before the family arose. She spent much of her day on her knees, while the footman spent his on his feet. At the height of the London season, a footman at Londonderry House once carried a pedometer all day. By the time he had finished work he had clocked up 18 miles (29 km), without leaving the house. Illustration from George R. Sims's 'Living London', 1901.*

servants might burn half a ton of coal in a day.

The fires gave out warmth, but they also gave out dust and dirt, and it was the housemaid's task to wage war against them, usually without any mechanical aid. Melville Bissell, the American inventor of a successful carpet sweeper, boasted in the 1880s that his device was 'in daily use in the households of HM the Queen and HRH the Princess of Wales', but in tens of thousands of homes carpets continued to be

Three picture postcards of domestic servants. Although produced after 1902, the two left-hand pictures illustrate the typical dress of parlour maids in the late Victorian period. The pair with the dog are probably from Cardiganshire, the young woman below left from east London. The motivation for such photographs is unclear. Some were no doubt paid for by the maids themselves, to send home. Others may have been taken by employers, as evidence of their servant-keeping status. A former nursemaid who was working in Palmers Green c.1908 later wrote: 'My employers didn't seem to have much money themselves; he was a clerk of some sort, but they liked the idea of having a "nurse-maid" and made me buy a cap, collar, cuffs and apron. Then the mistress took me to have a photograph taken with the children grouped around me.' The picture below right dates from 1915 and illustrates the shorter hemlines that were coming into vogue. (All three postcards: author's collection)

swept with a brush (one of dozens of specialist brushes to be found in a house), sometimes after damp tea leaves had been scattered on the floor to take up the dust. Before housewives began to do their own cleaning, labour-saving devices had comparatively little appeal. Instead, 'arm oil' and 'elbow grease' were advocated. It is surprising that 'housemaid's arm' and 'housemaid's elbow' did not join 'housemaid's knee' as a chronic ailment.

It was only by means of a strict routine that the work of cleaning a house could be accomplished. Each hour of the day and each day of the week had its clearly defined tasks. It was the housekeeper's responsibility to oversee all this activity, and to that end it was considered essential that she should possess the qualities of 'cleanliness, punctuality, order, and method'.

Many ladies' maids came from the ranks of dressmakers' assistants, since dress-

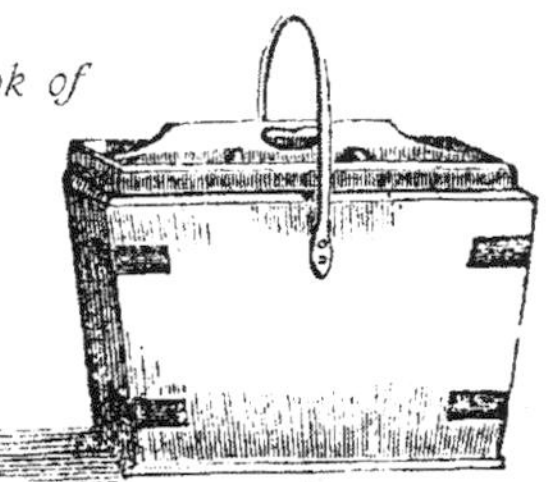

Right: *A housemaid's box, illustrated in Mrs Beeton's 'Book of Household Management'.*

Left: *Vast amounts of coal were consumed in Victorian homes. At Tatton a basement railway was installed to assist with the movement of coal scuttles. The ones on this trolley include the galvanised liners for the painted and crested scuttles that were used in family and guest rooms. (National Trust Photographic Library/Andreas von Einsiedel)*

POLISHING A PLEASURE!
STEPHENSON'S
WILL NOT FINGER MARK
FURNITURE CREAM
Sample Bottles Free by Post on Application.
SOLD BY CHEMISTS, GROCERS, IRONMONGERS, &c.
SOLE PROPRIETORS
STEPHENSON BROTHERS, Bradford.

Polishing might be a pleasure, but not to the extent that the mistress would ever contemplate doing it herself. Many proprietary brands of polish were available to domestic servants, although household manuals of the period were full of recipes for polishes and cleaning agents to be prepared at home. Advertisement from 'The Graphic', 11th July 1891.

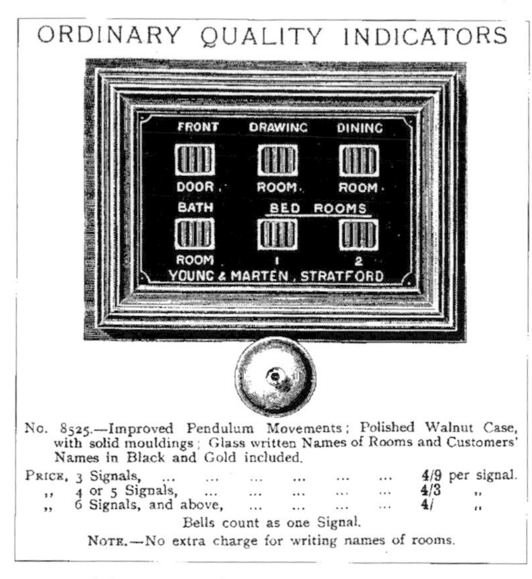

Like medieval monks and nuns, Victorian domestic servants led lives regulated by the sound of bells. Before the end of the eighteenth century it had become possible to fit houses with extensive systems of wire-operated bells and indicators, the work of bell-hanging often being undertaken by either plumbers or chimney sweeps. The facility of being able to summon servants from a distance was one of the factors that led to the increasing segregation of servants' quarters in larger houses. Advertisement from a trade catalogue of c.1897. (Reproduced by permission from 'The Victorian House Catalogue: Young and Martens', Sidgwick & Jackson.)

making, together with a knowledge of hairdressing, was an essential skill. The lady's maid helped her mistress to dress and undress and cared for her wardrobe. She spent much of her time in her mistress's company, so personal appearance and a pleasant manner were important. So too was youth, and as a lady's maid grew older she might find it harder to keep her place. Some made the transition to the role of housekeeper, but the chances of doing this were limited by a lack of knowledge of cookery and other aspects of domestic management, an omission that also affected a lady's maid's chances of marriage.

A knowledge of hairdressing was one of the expected skills of a lady's maid. Illustration from Mrs Beeton's 'Housewife's Treasury'.

KITCHEN AND LAUNDRY

As awesome as the butler was the cook. Good cooks always seem to have been in short supply, a fact of which they were well aware. The Edwardian writer H. H. Munro ('Saki') wrote of a cook who 'was a good cook, as cooks go; and as cooks go she went'. This was more than a neat play on words; it touched on a real anxiety for many mistresses. *The Servant's Practical Guide* commented that 'some ladies stand much in awe of their cooks, knowing that those who consider themselves thoroughly experienced will not brook fault-finding, or interference with their manner of cooking, and give notice to leave on the smallest pretext. Thus, when ladies obtain a really good cook, they deal with her delicately, and are inclined to let her have her own way with regard to serving the dinner.'

In the grandest establishments the cook was likely to be a man and to be even more temperamental. In his book *The Cook's Oracle* (1817), Dr William Kitchiner claimed that 'an English girl properly instructed can equal the best foreign gentlemen in everything except impudence and extravagance, and send up a delicious dinner with half the usual expense and trouble.' But even if this were true, she would not convey the same prestige, and the aristocracy continued to expect a chef to take charge of their kitchen.

Cooks in lesser households were either 'professed' cooks or 'plain' cooks, depending on the training they had received and the experience they could offer. In a small establishment the cook might find herself performing some of the general household duties and also preparing servants' meals. The larger the establishment, the more she could devote herself to her art. A 'professed' cook would do no cleaning, nor any of the plain cookery, and she would have ingredients prepared for her.

The busy times for a cook were the morning and the early evening. In the morning menus had to be agreed with the mistress; soups had to be made for the following day; pastries, jellies and other delicacies were prepared for the evening; and luncheon had to be cooked. From five until ten in the evening was a time of great activity, with nerves at their most tense. In the words of *The Servant's Practical Guide,* 'perfect silence is enjoined save when an order is given concerning the work in hand'. In reality, hot tempers as well as hot food must have abounded in many kitchens. After dinner had been served, the cook's work for the day was done, but the kitchen maids and scullery maids were left with the task of clearing up. Washing-up alone could be

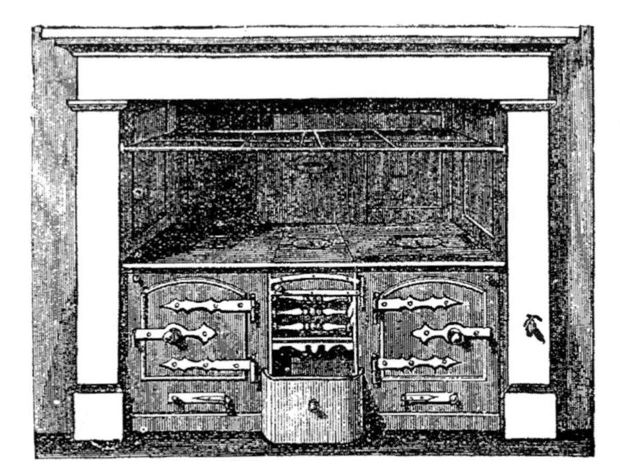

The Leamington Stove or 'Kitchener'. An engraving from Mrs Beeton's 'Book of Household Management', 1880 edition. The first patent for a closed iron range was taken out by an Exeter ironmonger in 1802, but the most successful early manufacturer was William Flavel of Leamington Spa in Warwickshire. It was he who coined the name 'kitchener' to convey the versatility of the enclosed range. In addition to the iron castings, which had to be blackleaded, there was often much brass and steel work that had to be kept constantly sparkling.

Right: *The Victorian craftsperson, whether in the workshop or the kitchen, expected to use equipment designed for very specific purposes, rather than multi-functional tools. The cook would thus expect her kitchen to be equipped with a wide range of pots and pans, each serving a particular function. It was usually some poor scullery maid who was expected to clean them all. Illustration from the 1881 edition of Mrs Beeton's 'Book of Household Management'.*

Above: *In 1882, in a comment on the spread of household gadgets, it was observed that 'This is a regular handle-turning age'. Kent's knife-cleaning machine (together with a rotary cinder-sifter) had been exhibited at the Crystal Palace some thirty years previously. Before the widespread use of stainless steel, the task of keeping cutlery clean was an arduous one for servants. Such 'Victorian' artefacts as this are still frequently found, although Kent's was producing an identical model as late as 1940. Advertisement from the 'Official Descriptive and Illustrated Catalogue of the Great Exhibition', 1851.*

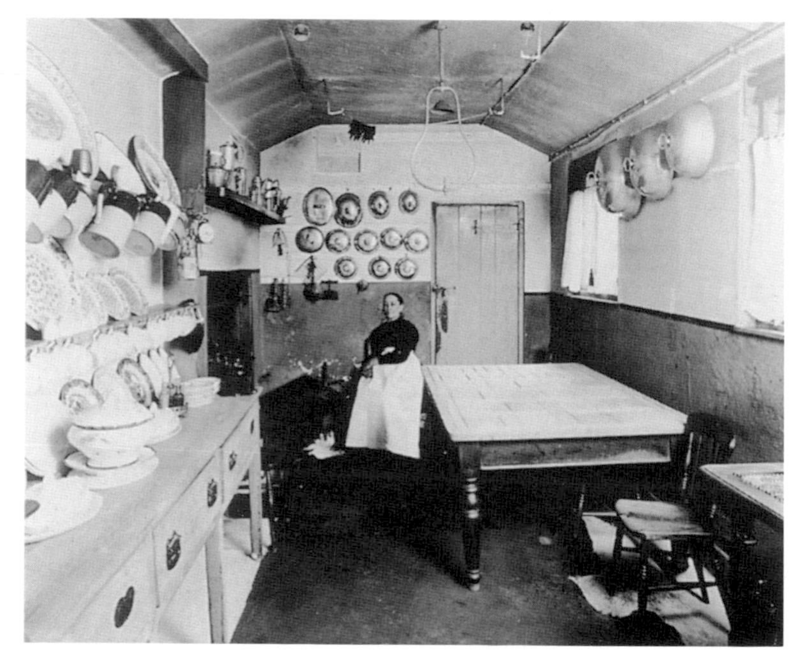

Left: *This picture indicates that the Victorian kitchen was not always the model of hygiene. The floor is covered with torn carpet, and the leg of the dresser is rotting away with damp. The ceiling is black with smoke, and paint peels from the walls. Yet the cook has brought order to her domain, and no doubt the food she is preparing is both wholesome and tasty. (London Metropolitan Archives)*

Right: *The royal kitchen in Windsor Castle, from the 'Illustrated London News', 28th December 1850. The number of staff employed in the kitchen at this time exceeded twenty. Subsequently, Queen Victoria employed several Indian cooks to produce curries, as well as an Egyptian coffee-maker. Gabriel Tschumi, a Swiss chef, started in the royal kitchens as an apprentice in 1898. He later wrote, 'I remember on my first day at Windsor thinking how much the kitchen reminded me of a chapel with its high domed ceiling'. The kitchen was indeed 50 feet (15 metres) in height, with lanterns in the roof to assist with ventilation. The Victorian kitchen might also be said to have resembled that other Victorian creation, the railway station, with its rising smoke and steam above and ordered efficiency below.*

Left: *The kitchen at Saltram House, Devon. Saltram is a Georgian house, built around the remnants of a Tudor mansion, and its 'Victorian' kitchen, like those in many country houses, contains elements spanning a broad period. The kitchen itself was built in 1780. The open range at the back was installed c.1810, while the great Leamington kitchener in the middle of the room dates from 1885. Saltram has a spacious scullery, with impressive coppers for boiling vegetables, hams or puddings, which could be used as a kitchen when the family was absent or only a small amount of cooking had to be done. (National Trust Photographic Library/Rob Matheson)*

The kitchen of Minley Manor, Hampshire (built 1858-62 for a partner in Glynn Mills bank), photographed in the 1890s. The construction and fitting-out of a large kitchen involved considerable expense, and this room was generally the only one occupied by servants that architects and owners bothered to photograph. (RCHME. © Crown Copyright)

Right: *Wooden sinks were often installed in larger houses in order to minimise the chance of breaking expensive china or glassware. Items of considerable value passed through a servant's hands, and (at least where relations between master and servant were good) it was a matter of professional pride to take care. One head housemaid was able to claim not to have broken or chipped a single object during twenty-five years of service, and she was probably not alone in this. These deep teak sinks are at Tatton Park, Cheshire. (National Trust Photographic Library/ Andreas von Einsiedel)*

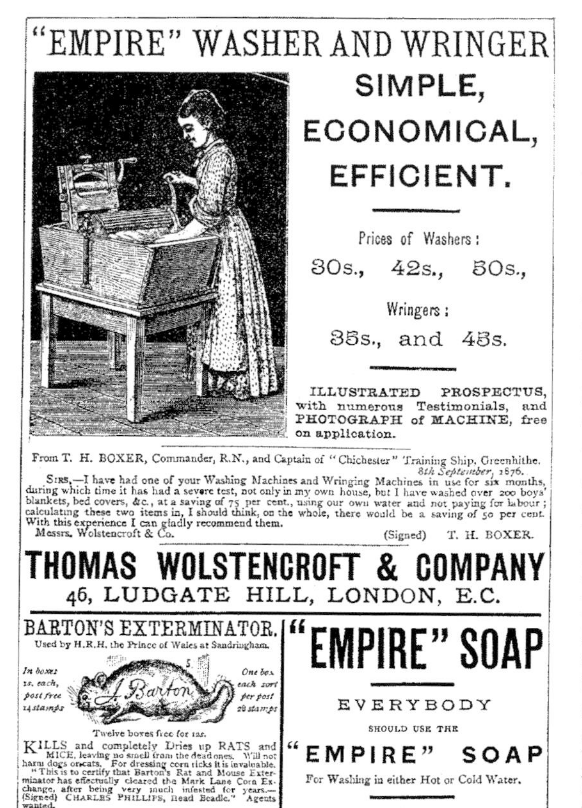

Below: *Patents for washing machines appeared as early as the 1750s, but it was not until the mid nineteenth century that machines of any serious practical use appeared. The one shown here was advertised in 'Whitaker's Almanack' in 1878.*

a formidable task, as a full-length dinner for eighteen people might well generate five hundred separate items of glassware, china, cutlery and kitchenware to be cleaned.

A large house produced not only mountains of washing-up but also large volumes of laundry. How this was dealt with depended partly on location. On country estates it was much more likely that laundry would be done 'in house', since there was plenty of outdoor space available for the drying and bleaching of clothes. In earlier times hedges of lavender and rosemary were even grown, for the specific purpose of imparting a pleasant smell to the drying clothes hung on them. Country houses were usually equipped with separate laundry rooms, which, because of the amount of steam, smell and moisture they produced and because they needed to be near the drying ground, were often in a separate self-contained location. Laundry maids tended to be an independent group, not always under the control of the housekeeper. Their proximity to the groom-filled stables was recognised as a problem by some employers. At Packenham Hall in Ireland the laundry was linked to the drying ground by an underground passage (installed in the 1840s), which ran the length of the stables and reduced the chance of laun-

Left and below: *'You'll never regret employing such a perfect cook as the VALOR-PERFECTION Oil Cooking Stove', claims this housewife in 1922. After the First World War human cooks were hard to find. However, with a little help from such products as Mackintosh's Toffee-de-Luxe even housework could supposedly be made fun. Advertisements from 'Good Housekeeping', March 1922.*

dry maids meeting stable-lads.

As early as 1861, Mrs Beeton was referring to the growing practice in towns of sending laundry out to professional laundresses and laundry companies. In 1873 a writer on country houses described laundry work as 'hardly economical'. The development of highly mechanised commercial laundering (together with that of motor transport, which facilitated collection and delivery) led to a sharp decline in the number of laundry maids in the period before the First World War.

THE DECLINE OF DOMESTIC SERVICE

The employment statistics relating to domestic service are difficult to interpret, and it has been argued that the number of people employed in this field reached its highest in the 1870s, somewhat earlier than was once believed. However, what was happening to laundry work seems to reflect a development towards the relocation of domestic chores outside the home. This in turn led to a shift in status for women workers. An employee in a steam laundry was not in the same position as a laundry maid. The one had freedom; the other did not.

The First World War set the seal on this process of change. It marked the beginning of a technological age, which would lead to the evolution of the labour-saving home, equipped with newly-invented devices. 'The house-proud woman in these days of servant shortage does not always know the best ways to lessen her own burdens', wrote *Good Housekeeping* in its first issue (March 1922). But she would soon learn.

Pictures of the Victorian nursery are often idealised images of peace and tranquillity, but this engraving from 'The Graphic', 27th February 1875, conveys a quite different message. It was not for nothing that nurseries were often placed at the top of the house, as far away from the family as possible.

FURTHER READING

The following books are listed in alphabetical order of author's surname. That is the way the writer intended; and that is the way they should be left. For, as 'A Lady' wrote in her *Common Sense for Housemaids* (1850), 'A housemaid should never exercise her own taste in arranging books in a gentleman's study.'

Acton, Eliza. *Modern Cookery for Private Families.* First published in 1855; reissued in facsimile with an introduction by Elizabeth Ray, Southover Press, 1993.

Adams, Samuel and Sarah. *The Complete Servant.* First published in 1825; reissued in facsimile with an introduction by Pamela Horn, Southover Press, 2000.

Anon. *The Servant's Practical Guide.* Frederick Warne, 1880.

Beeton, Mrs Isabella. *The Book of Household Management.* First published in book form by S. O. Beeton, 1861. There have been numerous reprints, including some in facsimile. A recent edition, with an introduction by Nicola Humble, was published by Oxford University Press in 2000.

Booth, Charles. *Life and Labour of the People in London* (volume 8). Macmillan, 1896.

Burnett, John. *Useful Toil.* Allen Lane, 1974.

Calder, Jenni. *The Victorian Home.* Batsford, 1977.

Dawes, Frank Victor. *Not in Front of the Servants.* Century, 1989.

Drury, Elizabeth. *Victorian Household Hints.* Past Times, 1996.

Ereira, Alan. *The People's England.* Routledge & Kegan Paul, 1981.

Flanders, Judith.*The Victorian House.* Harper Collins, 2004.

French, Anne, and Waterfield, Giles (editors). *Below Stairs: 400 Years of Servants' Portraits.* National Portrait Gallery, 2003.

Gathorne-Hardy, Jonathan. *The Rise and Fall of the British Nanny.* Hodder & Stoughton, 1972.

Girouard, Mark. *Life in the English Country House.* Yale, 1978.

Girouard, Mark. *The Victorian Country House.* Yale, 1979.

Hardyment, Christina. *Behind the Scenes. Domestic Arrangements in Historic Houses.* National Trust, 1997.

Hartup, Adeline. *Below Stairs in the Great Country Houses.* Sidgwick & Jackson, 1980.

Horn, Pamela. *The Rise and Fall of the Victorian Servant.* Alan Sutton, 1995.

Horn, Pamela. *Life below Stairs in the Twentieth Century.* Alan Sutton, 2001.

Hudson, Derek. *Munby: Man of Two Worlds.* Abacus, 1974.

Huggett, Frank. *Life Below Stairs.* John Murray, 1977.

Hughes, Kathryn. *The Short Life and Long Times of Mrs Beeton.* Fourth Estate, 2005.

Lochhead, Marion. *The Victorian Household.* John Murray, 1964.

Stuart, Dorothy M. *The English Abigail.* Macmillan, 1946.

Turner, E.S. *What the Butler Saw.* Michael Joseph, 1982.

A number of other Shire Albums have a bearing on the history of domestic service, including *Old Cooking Utensils* and *Firegrates and Kitchen Ranges*, both by David J. Eveleigh, and *Domestic Bygones* by Jacqueline Fearn.

PLACES TO VISIT

The following town and country houses make a special feature of their domestic arrangements:

Calke Abbey, Ticknall, Derby DE73 7LE. Telephone: 01332 863822. National Trust.

Carlyle's House, 24 Cheyne Row, Chelsea, London SW3 5HL. Telephone 020 7352 7087. National Trust.

Castle Ward, Strangford, Downpatrick, County Down BT30 7LS. Telephone: 02844 881204. National Trust.

Cragside House, Rothbury, Morpeth, Northumberland NE65 7PX. Telephone: 01669 620333. National Trust.

The Darby Houses (Rosehill and Dale House), Darby Road, Coalbrookdale, Telford, Shropshire TF8 7EW. Telephone: 01952 884391. Website: www.ironbridge.org.uk
Dunham Massey, Altrincham, Cheshire WA14 4SJ. Telephone: 0161 941 1025. National Trust.
Erddig, near Wrexham LL13 0YT. Telephone: 01978 315151; 'infoline' 01978 315151. National Trust.
Holker Hall, Cark-in-Cartmel, Grange-over-Sands, Cumbria LA11 7PL. Telephone: 01539 558328. Website: www.holker-hall.co.uk
Kingston Lacy, Wimborne Minster, Dorset BH21 4EA. Telephone: 01202 883402. National Trust.
Lanhydrock, Bodmin, Cornwall PL30 5AD. Telephone: 01208 625950. National Trust.
Longleat House, Warminster, Wiltshire BA12 7NW. Telephone: 01985 844400. Website: www.longleat.co.uk
Lyme Park, Disley, Stockport, Cheshire SK12 2NR. Telephone: 01663 762023; 'infoline' 01663 766492. National Trust.
Manderston, Duns, Berwickshire TD11 3PP. Telephone: 01361 883450. Website: www.manderston.co.uk
Newbridge House, Donabate, County Dublin, Republic of Ireland. Telephone: 00353 1 8436534.
Petworth House, Petworth, West Sussex GU28 0AE. Telephone: 01798 342207; 'infoline' 01798 343929. National Trust.
Shugborough Estate, Milford, Stafford ST17 0XB. Telephone: 01889 881388. National Trust. Website: www.shugborough.org.uk
Tatton Park, Knutsford, Cheshire WA16 6QN. Telephone: 01625 374400. National Trust. Website: www.tattonpark.org.uk
Thirlestane Castle, Lauder, Berwickshire TD2 6RU. Telephone: 01578 722430. Website: www.thirlestanecastle.co.uk
Uppark, South Harting, Petersfield, West Sussex GU31 5QR. Telephone: 01730 825415; 'infoline' 01730 825857. National Trust.

For information about National Trust properties, the Trust's website is www.nationaltrust.org.uk

Many museums with social history displays contain relevant material, including the following:

Bygones at Holkham, Holkham Park, Wells next the Sea, Norfolk NR23 1AB. Telephone: 01328 710227. Website: www.holkham.co.uk
Worcestershire County Museum, Hartlebury Castle, Hartlebury, Kidderminster, Worcestershire DY11 7XZ. Telephone: 01299 250416. Website: www.worcestershire.gov.uk
Grosvenor Museum, 27 Grosvenor Street, Chester, Cheshire CH1 2DD. Telephone: 01244 402008. Website: www.chestercc.gov.uk
The Royal Pavilion, 4/5 Pavilion Buildings, Brighton, East Sussex BN1 1EE. Telephone: 0300 0290900. Website: www.royalpavilion.org.uk
St John's House Museum, St John's, Warwick CV34 4NF. Telephone: 01926 412021. Website: www.warwickshire.gov.uk
Science Museum, Exhibition Road, South Kensington, London SW7 2DD. Telephone: 0870 870 4868. Website: www.sciencemuseum.org.uk
York Castle Museum, Eye of York, York YO1 9RY. Telephone: 01904 687687. Website: www.yorkcastlemuseum.org.uk